I0568918

SWU-700-008

UNIFORMS OF RUSSIAN ARMY OF ELIZABETH OF RUSSIA VOL.2

UNDER THE REIGN OF ELIZABETH PETROVNA FROM 1741 TO 1761, AND PETER III FROM 1762

From the Viskovatov's greatest work:
"Historical description of the clothing and
arms of the Russian Army"

SOLDIERSHOP PUBLISHING

AUTHOR

Aleksandr Vasilevich Viskovatov born 22 April (4 May New Style) 1804, died 27 February (11 March) 1858 in St. Petersburg, Russian military historian. He graduated from the 1st Cadet Corps and served in the artillery, the hydrographic depot of the Naval Ministry, and then in the Department of Military Educational Institutions. He mainly studied historical artifacts and the histories of military units. Viskovatov's greatest work was the Historical Description of the Clothing and Arms of the Russian Army.

Title: **UNIFORMS OF RUSSIAN ARMY OF ELIZABETH OF RUSSIA VOL. 2 -**
Under the reign of Elizabeth Petrovna from 1741 to 1761 and Peter III from 1762
By A.V.Viskovatov. Serie edit by Luca S. Cristini. First edition by Soldiershop. February 2018
Cover & Art Design: Luca S. Cristini. Plates re-colorations by Anna Cristini.
ISBN code: 978-88-93273190

Published by Soldiershop publishing, via Padre Davide, 7 - 24050 Zanica (BG) ITALY. www.soldiershop.com

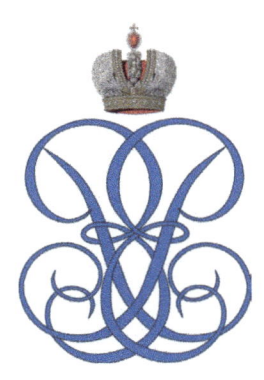

UNIFORMS
OF THE RUSSIAN ARMY OF
ELIZABETH OF RUSSIA
1741-1762
VOL. 2

UNDER THE REIGN OF ELIZABETH PETROVNA
FROM 1741 TO 1761 AND PETER III FROM 1762

HISTORICAL DESCRIPTION OF THE CLOTHING AND ARMS
OF THE RUSSIAN ARMY - A.V. VISKOVATOV

Soldiershop is glad to presents the complete collection of the great job made by A.V. Viskovatov dedicated to the uniforms and weapons belonging from the first Zar and Russian emperors to the Russian army during the Napoleonic period, until 1860 about. The time we considered in this volume corresponds to the reigns of of the Duke of Courland and Princess Anna of Braunschweig-Luneburg from 1740 to 1741, Empress Elizabeth Petrovna from 1741 to 1761, and Emperor Peter III from 1762.

Our new edition, the first ever published in English, both on paper and digital format, boasts a large number of color plates, many of them unpublished and re-coloured by our team of expert artists and scholars of uniformology. Each volume is based on 100 color plates or more, always accompanied by the original translated text which describes the subjects of the plates.

A unique work in its genre, a must have in any respecting collection!

Aleksandr Vasilevich Viskovatov born 22 April (4 May New Style) 1804, died 27 February (11 March) 1858 in St. Petersburg, Russian military historian. He graduated from the 1st Cadet Corps and served in the artillery, the hydrographic depot of the Naval Ministry, and then in the Department of Military Educational Institutions.

He mainly studied historical artifacts and the histories of military units. Viskovatov's greatest work was the Historical Description of the Clothing and Arms of the Russian Army (Vols. 1-30, St. Petersburg, 1841-62; 2nd ed. Vols. 1-34, St. Petersburg - Novosibirsk - Leningrad, 1899-1948). This work is based on a great quantity of archival documents and contains four thousand colored illustrations.

Viskovatov was the author of Chronicles of the Russian Army (Books 1-20, St. Petersburg, 1834-42) and Chronicles of the Russian Imperial Army (Parts 1-7, St. Petersburg, 1852). He collected valuable material on the history of the Russian navy which went into A Short Overview of Russian Naval Campaigns and General Voyages to the End of the XVII Century (St. Petersburg, 1864; 2nd edition Moscow, 1946). Together with A.I. Mikhailovskii-Danilevskii he helped prepare and create the Military Gallery in the Winter Palace.

He wrote the historical military inscriptions for the walls of the Hall of St. George in the Great Palace of the Kremlin. (From the article in the Soviet Military Encyclopedia.)

◄ *Elizabeth of Russia in a portrait by anonymous (1745 about)*

CONTENTS

HISTORICAL DESCRIPTION OF THE RUSSIAN EMPRESS ELIZABETH PETROVNA 1709-1762

Elizabeth Petrovna (29 December 1709 – 5 January 1762), also known as **Yelisaveta** or **Elizaveta**, was the Empress of Russia from 1741 until her death.

She led the country during the two major European conflicts of her time: the War of Austrian Succession (1740–48) and the Seven Years' War (1756–63). Her domestic policies allowed the nobles to gain dominance in local government while shortening their terms of service to the state. She encouraged Mikhail Lomonosov's establishment of the University of Moscow and Ivan Shuvalov's foundation of the Imperial Academy of Arts in Saint Petersburg.

She also spent exorbitant sums of money on the grandiose baroque projects of her favourite architect, Bartolomeo Rastrelli, particularly in Peterhof and Tsarskoye Selo. The Winter Palace and the Smolny Cathedral in Saint Petersburg are among the chief monuments of her reign.

She remains one of the most popular Russian monarchs due to her strong opposition to Prussian policies and her decision not to execute a single person during her reign.

EARLY LIFE

Elizabeth was born at Kolomenskoye, near Moscow, the daughter of Peter the Great, Tsar of Russia, by his second wife, Catherine I. Catherine had been a maid in the household of Peter the Great and, although no documentary record exists, they are said to have married secretly at the Cathedral of the Holy Trinity in St. Petersburg at some point of time between 23 October and 1 December 1707. Peter valued Catherine and married her again (this time officially) at Saint Isaac's Cathedral in St. Petersburg on 9 February 1712.

On this day, the two children previously born to them (Anna and Elizabeth) were legitimized by their father. The circumstances of Elizabeth's birth would later be used by her political opponents to challenge her right to the throne on grounds of illegitimate birth.

Of the twelve children born to Peter and Catherine (five sons and seven daughters), only two daughters, Anna (b. 1708) and Elizabeth (b. 1709,) survived to adulthood. Both of them were given the title of Tsarevna ("princess") on 6 March 1711, and of Tsesarevna ("crown princess") on 23 December 1721. They had one older surviving sibling, crown prince Alexei Petrovich, who was Peter's son by his first wife Eudoxia Lopukhina, a noblewoman.

As a child, Elizabeth was the particular favorite of her father. She resembled him both physically and temperamentally. She was a bright girl, if not brilliant, but received only a desultory formal education. Even though he adored his daughter, Peter did not devote time or attention to her education. He had a son (and grandson) from his first marriage to a noblewoman, and did not anticipate that a daughter born to his former maid and second wife might one day inherit the throne.

Indeed, no woman had ever sat upon the throne of Russia yet. It was therefore left to Catherine to raise the girls as best she could, but she was herself too uneducated to be able to superintend the formal education of her daughters. Elizabeth had a French governess and grew fluent in Italian, German and French. She was also an excellent dancer and rider. Like her father, Elizabeth was physically active and loved riding, hunting, sledging, skating, and gardening.

From her earliest years, she delighted everyone with her extraordinary beauty and vivacity, and was regarded as the leading beauty of the Russian Empire.[2] The wife of the British minister (ambassador) described Elizabeth as "fair, with light brown hair, large sprightly blue eyes, fine teeth and a pretty mouth. She is inclinable to be fat, but is very genteel and dances better than anyone I ever saw. She speaks German, French and Italian, is extremely gay and talks to everyone…"

MARRIAGE PLANS AND PERSONAL LIFE

Peter was enamored of western Europe, and much of his fame rests on his efforts to westernize Russia. A corollary to this proclivity was his desire to see his children married into the royal houses of Europe, something which his predecessors had actually avoided.

Peter's only son and heir was born of his first marriage to a nobleman's daughter, and no problem was encountered in securing a bride for him from the ancient house of Brunswick-Lüneburg.

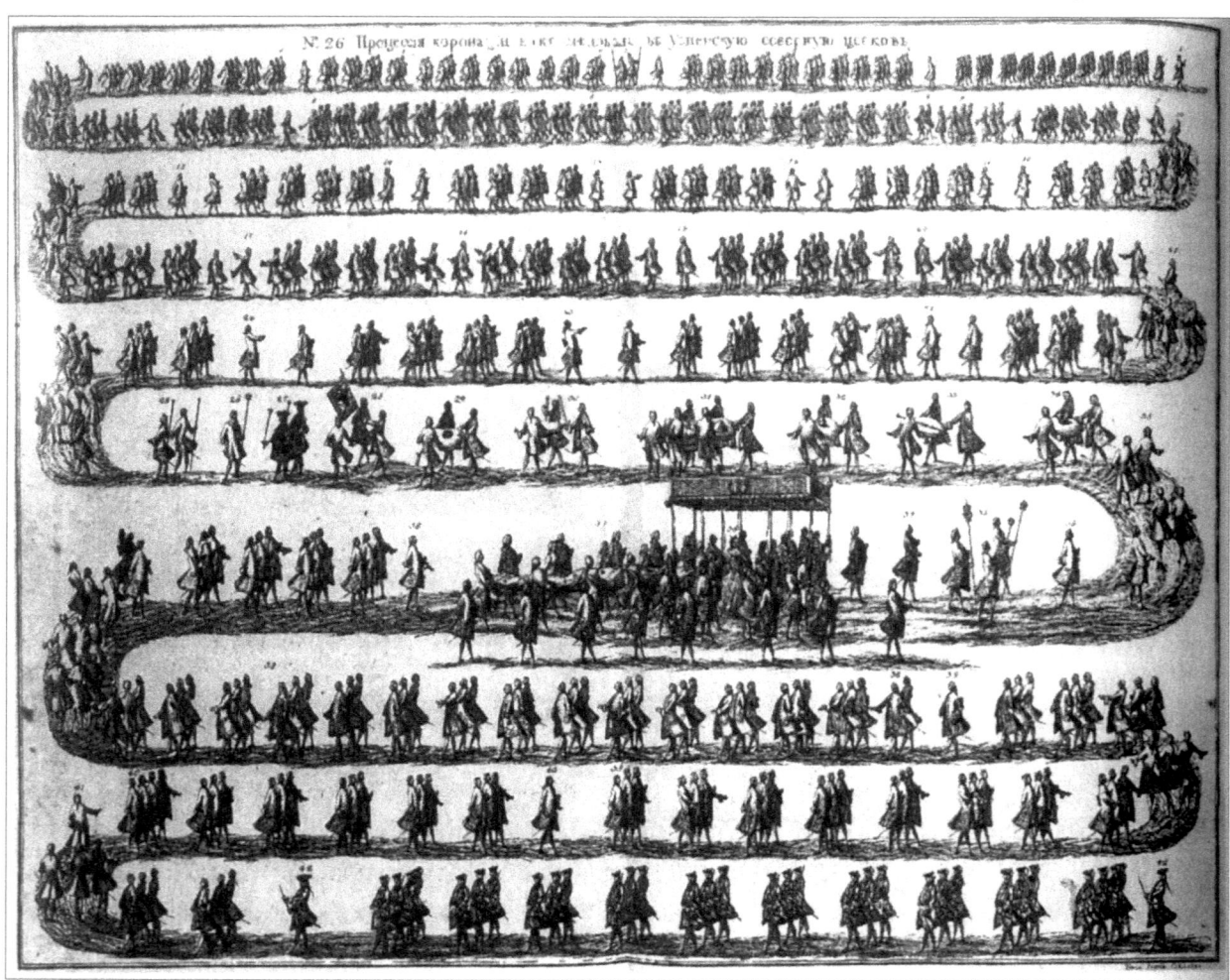

The Coronation Procession of Elisabeth of Russia by Ivan Sokolow

However, Peter was hard put to arrange similar marriages for the daughters born of his second wife, who had formerly been a maid in his household. He was roundly snubbed by the Bourbons of France when, during a visit to that country, he offered either of his daughters in marriage to the future Louis XV. The French court conveyed to him in brief that the antecedents of the girls' mother was unacceptable.

In 1724, Peter betrothed his daughters to two young princes, first cousins to each other, who hailed from the tiny north German principality of Holstein-Gottorp, and whose family was undergoing a period of political and economic stress. Anna Petrovna (aged 16) was to marry Charles Frederick, Duke of Holstein-Gottorp, who was then living in exile in Russia as Peter's guest after having failed in his attempt to succeed his maternal uncle as King of Sweden, and whose patrimony (Holstein-Gottorp) was at that time under Danish occupation.

Despite all this, the prince was of impeccable birth and well-connected to many royal houses; it seemed a politically useful and respectable alliance, and Peter was happy. Some time later, Elizabeth was betrothed to marry Charles Frederick's first cousin, Charles Augustus of Holstein-Gottorp, the eldest son of Christian Augustus, Prince of Eutin.

Anna's wedding was held in 1725 as planned, even though Peter died a few weeks before the nuptials. In Elizabeth's case, however, her fiancé died on 31 May 1727, before the wedding could be held.

Unfortunately, Elizabeth's mother Catherine I (who had succeeded Peter the Great to the throne) also died on 17 May 1727, just two weeks before Elizabeth's fiancé.

Thus, by the end of May 1727, Elizabeth (aged 17) had lost her fiance and both of her parents; and furthermore, her half-nephew Peter II was on the throne. Her marriage prospects immediately dried up. They did not improve when, three years later, Peter II died and was succeeded by Elizabeth's first cousin, Empress Anna (ruled 1730-40), daughter of Peter the Great's elder brother Ivan V. There was little love lost between the cousins and no prospect of either any Russian nobleman or any foreign prince seeking Elizabeth's hand in marriage.

Nor could Elizabeth marry a commoner because it would cost her not only her title and royal status, but also her property rights and her claim to the throne. The fact that Elizabeth was something of a beauty did not bring her any advantage in marriage prospects; on the other hand, it earned her some resentment. When the Chinese minister in St. Petersburg was asked by the Empress Anna who was the most beautiful woman at her court, he pointed to Elizabeth, to Anna's intense displeasure. Elizabeth's response to the lack of marriage prospects was to take Alexis Shubin, a handsome sergeant in the Semyonovsky Guards regiment, as her lover.

When Empress Anna found out about this, Shubin's tongue was cut off and he was banished to Siberia. Elizabeth consoled herself with a handsome coachman and then turned to a footman for her sexual pleasure. Eventually she found her long-term companion in Alexis Razumovsky, a young and handsome Ukrainian peasant serf with a good bass voice.

Razumovsky had been brought from his village to St. Petersburg by his master, a nobleman, to sing for a church choir. Elizabeth purchased the talented serf from the nobleman for her own choir. Razumovsky, a good-hearted and simple-minded man, never evidenced any personal ambition or interest in affairs of state during all the years of his relationship with Elizabeth which spanned from the days of her obscurity to the height of her power as Empress. In turn, Elizabeth was devoted to Razumovsky, and there is reason to believe that she might even have married him in a secret ceremony. Razumovsky would later become known as "the Emperor of the Night." In 1756, Elizabeth would make him a Prince and a Field Marshal. In 1742, the Holy Roman Emperor made Razumovsky a Count of the Holy Roman Empire.

YEARS OF OBSCURITY

So long as Aleksandr Danilovich Menshikov remained in power (until September 1727) the government of Elizabeth's adolescent half-nephew Peter II (reigned 1727-1730) treated her with liberality and distinction. The Dolgorukovs, an ancient boyar family, deeply resented Menshikov.
With Peter II's attachment to Prince Ivan Dolgorukov, and with two of their family members on the Supreme State Council, they had the leverage for a successful *coup*.
Menshikov was arrested, stripped of all his honours and properties and exiled to northern Siberia where he died in November 1729. The Dolgorukovs hated the memory of Peter the Great and practically banished his daughter from Court. During the reign of her cousin, Anna (1730–1740), Elizabeth was gathering support in the background.
After the death of Empress Anna, the regency of Anna Leopoldovna for the infant Ivan VI was marked by high taxes and economic problems.
Elizabeth, being the daughter of Peter the Great, enjoyed much support from the Russian guards regiments. The French ambassador in St. Petersburg, the marquis de La Chétardie was deeply involved in planning a coup to depose the regent Anna whose anti-French foreign policy was opposed to the interests of France, and bribed numerous officers in the Imperial Guard to support the coup.
Elizabeth often visited the elite Guards regiments, marking special events with the officers, and acting as godmother to their children.

SEIZING POWER

The guards repaid her kindness when, on the night of 25 November 1741, Elizabeth seized power with the help of the Preobrazhensky Regiment. Arriving at the regimental headquarters wearing a warrior's metal breastplate over her dress and grasping a silver cross she challenged them: "Whom do you want to serve: me, your natural sovereign, or those who have stolen my inheritance?"
Won over, the regiment marched to the Winter Palace and arrested the infant Emperor, his parents, and their own lieutenant-colonel, Count von Munnich. It was a daring coup and, amazingly, succeeded without bloodshed. Elizabeth had vowed that if she became Empress she would not sign a single death sentence, an extraordinary promise for the time but one which she kept throughout her life.

DOMESTIC POLICY

At the age of thirty-three, with relatively little political experience, Elizabeth found herself at the head of a great empire at one of the most critical periods of its existence.
Her proclamation as Empress Elizabeth I explained that the preceding reigns had led Russia to ruin: "The Russian people have been groaning under the enemies of the Christian faith, but she has delivered them from the degrading foreign oppression."
Russia had been under the domination of German advisers and Elizabeth exiled the most unpopular of them, including Heinrich Ostermann, Burkhard von Munnich and Carl Gustav Lowenwolde. Elizabeth crowned herself Empress in the Dormition Cathedral on 25 April 1742. Fortunately for her-

Elizabeth in his palace at Zarkoie Tzelo painting by Eugene Lanceray, now in the Tretyakov Gallery.

self and for Russia, Elizabeth Petrovna, with all her shortcomings (documents often waited months for her signature), had inherited some of her father's genius for government. Her usually keen judgment and her diplomatic tact again and again recalled Peter the Great. What sometimes appeared as irresolution and procrastination was most often a wise suspension of judgment under exceptionally difficult circumstances.

The substantial changes made by Elizabeth's father, Peter the Great, had not exercised a really formative influence on the intellectual attitudes of the ruling classes as a whole. Elizabeth made considerable impact and laid the groundwork for its completion by her eventual successor, Catherine II.

FOREIGN POLICY

Elizabeth abolished the cabinet council system that had been used under Anna, and reconstituted the senate as it had been under Peter the Great with the chiefs of the departments of state (none of them Germans) attending. Her first task after this was to address the war with Sweden. On 23 January 1743 direct negotiations between the two powers were opened at Åbo (Turku). In the Treaty of Åbo, on 7 August 1743, Sweden ceded to Russia all of southern Finland east of the Kymmene River, which became the boundary between the two states. The treaty also gave Russia the fortresses of Villmanstrand and Fredrikshamn. This triumphant issue can be credited to the diplomatic ability of the new vice chancellor, Aleksey Bestuzhev-Ryumin. His policies would have been impossible without her support. Elizabeth had wisely placed Bestuzhev at the head of foreign affairs immediately after her accession. He represented the anti-Franco-Prussian portion of her council, and his object was to bring about an Anglo-Austro-Russian alliance which, at that time, was undoubtedly Russia's proper system.

Hence the bogus Lopukhina Conspiracy and other attempts of Frederick the Great and Louis XV to get rid of Bestuzhev failed, but it put the Russian court into the centre of a tangle of intrigue during the earlier years of Elizabeth's reign).

Ultimately the minister's strong support from Elizabeth prevailed. His faultless diplomacy, and an auxiliary Russian corps of 30,000 men sent to the Rhine, greatly accelerated the peace negotiations leading to the treaty of Aix-la-Chapelle (18 October 1748).

By sheer tenacity of purpose Bestuzhev had extricated his country from the Swedish imbroglio; reconciled his imperial mistress with the courts of Vienna and London; enabled Russia to assert herself effectually in Poland, Turkey and Sweden; and isolated the King of Prussia by forcing him into hostile alliances. All this would have been impossible without the steady support of Elizabeth who trusted him completely in spite of the Chancellor's many enemies, most of whom were her personal friends.

However, on 14 February 1758, Chancellor Bestuzhev was removed from office. The future Catherine II recorded, CHe was relieved of all his decorations and rank, without a soul being able to reveal for what crimes or transgressions the first gentleman of the Empire was so despoiled, and sent back to his house as a prisoner." No specific crime was ever pinned on Bestuzhev.

Instead it was inferred that he had attempted to sow discord between the Empress and her heir and his consort. Enemies of pro-Austrian Bestuzhev were his rivals; the Shuvalov family, Vice-Chancellor Mikhail Vorontsov, and the French ambassador.

SEVEN-YEARS WAR

The great event of Elizabeth's later years was the Seven Years' War. Elizabeth regarded the treaty of Westminster (16 January 1756, whereby Great Britain and Prussia agreed to unite their forces to oppose the entry into, or the passage through, Germany of the troops of every foreign power) as utterly subversive of the previous conventions between Great Britain and Russia. Elizabeth sided against Prussia over a personal dislike of Frederick the Great.

She wanted him reduced within proper limits so that he might no longer be a danger to the empire. Elizabeth acceded to the treaty of Versailles thus entering into an alliance with France and Austria against Prussia. On 17 May 1757 the Russian army, 85,000 strong, advanced against Königsberg. Neither the serious illness of the Empress, which began with a fainting-fit at Tsarskoe Selo (19 September 1757), nor the fall of Bestuzhev (21 February 1758), nor the cabals and intrigues of the various foreign powers at Saint Petersburg, interfered with the progress of the war, and the crushing defeat of Kunersdorf (12 August 1759) at last brought Frederick to the verge of ruin. From that day forth he despaired of success, though he was saved for the moment by the jealousies of the Russian and Austrian commanders which ruined the military plans of the allies. On the other hand, it is not too much to say that, from the end of 1759 to the end of 1761, the unshakable firmness of the Russian Empress was the one constraining political force which held together the heterogeneous, incessantly jarring elements of the anti-Prussian combination.

From the Russian point of view Elizabeth's greatness as a stateswoman consists in her steady appreciation of Russian interests, and her determination to promote them at all hazards. She insisted throughout that the King of Prussia must be rendered harmless to his neighbors for the future, and that the only way to bring this about was to reduce him to the rank of a Prince-Elector.

Frederick himself was quite alive to his danger. "I'm at the end of my resources," he wrote at the beginning of 1760, "the continuance of this war means for me utter ruin. Things may drag on perhaps till July, but then a catastrophe must come." On 21 May 1760 a fresh convention was signed between Russia and Austria, a secret clause of which, never communicated to the court of Versailles, guaranteed East Prussia to Russia as an indemnity for war expenses.

The failure of the campaign of 1760, wielded by the inept Count Buturlin, induced the court of Versailles, on the evening of 22 January 1761, to present to the court of Saint Petersburg a dispatch to the effect that the king of France, by reason of the condition of his dominions, absolutely desired peace. The Russian empress's reply was delivered to the two ambassadors on 12 February.

It was inspired by the most uncompromising hostility towards the king of Prussia. Elizabeth would not consent to any pacific overtures until the original object of the league had been accomplished. Simultaneously Elizabeth had conveyed to Louis XV a confidential letter in which she proposed the signature of a new treaty of alliance of a more comprehensive and explicit nature than the preceding treaties between the two powers without the knowledge of Austria.

Elizabeth's object in this mysterious negotiation seems to have been to reconcile France and Great Britain, in return for which signal service France was to throw all her forces into the German war. This project, which lacked neither ability nor audacity, foundered upon Louis XV's invincible jealousy of the growth of Russian influence in eastern Europe and his fear of offending the Porte.

It was finally arranged by the allies that their envoys at Paris should fix the date for the assembling of a peace congress, and that, in the meantime, the war against Prussia should be vigorously prosecuted. In 1760 a Russian flying column briefly occupied Berlin. Russian victories placed Prussia in serious danger. The campaign of 1761 was almost as abortive as the campaign of 1760. Frederick acted on the defensive with consummate skill, and the capture of the Prussian fortress of Kolberg on Christmas Day 1761, by Rumyantsev, was the sole Russian success. Frederick, however, was now at the last gasp.

On 6 January 1762 he wrote to Count Karl-Wilhelm Finck von Finckenstein, "We ought now to think of preserving for my nephew, by way of negotiation, whatever fragments of my territory we can save from the avidity of my enemies," which means, if words mean anything, that he was resolved to seek a soldier's death on the first opportunity. A fortnight later he wrote to Prince Ferdinand of Brunswick, "The sky begins to clear. Courage, my dear fellow. I have received the news of a great event."

The great event which snatched him from destruction was the death of the Russian empress (5 January 1762 (N.S.)).

SELECTING AN HEIR

As an unmarried and childless empress, it was imperative for Elizabeth to find a legitimate heir to secure the Romanov dynasty. She chose her nephew, Peter of Holstein-Gottorp. Elizabeth was only too aware that the deposed Ivan VI, whom she had imprisoned in the Schlusselburg Fortress and placed in solitary confinement, was a threat to her throne. Elizabeth feared a coup in his favour and set about destroying all papers, coins or anything else depicting or mentioning Ivan. Elizabeth had issued an order that, should any attempt be made for him to escape, he was to be eliminated. Catherine II upheld the order and when an attempt was made he was killed and secretly buried within the fortress. The young Peter had lost his mother, Elizabeth's sister Anna, at three months old and his father at the age of eleven. Elizabeth invited her young nephew to Saint Petersburg where he was received into the Orthodox Church and proclaimed heir on 7 November 1742.

Elizabeth gave him at once Russian tutors. Keen to see the dynasty secured Elizabeth settled on Princess Sophie of Anhalt-Zerbst as a bride for her nephew. Incidentally, Sophie's mother, Joanna Elisabeth of Holstein-Gottorp, was a sister of Elizabeth's own fiancé who had died before the wedding. On her conversion to the Russian Orthodox Church Sophie was given the name 'Catherine' in memory of Elizabeth's mother. The marriage took place on 21 August 1745.

Nine years later, a son, the future Paul I, was finally born on 20 September 1754. There is considerable speculation as to the actual paternity of Paul I. It is suggested that he was not Peter's son at all, but that his mother had engaged in an affair—to which Elizabeth had consented—with a young officer named Sergei Vasilievich Saltykov, and that he was Paul's real father. In any case Peter never gave any indication that he believed Paul to have been fathered by anyone but himself. He also did not take any interest in parenthood. Elizabeth though most certainly took an active interest. She removed the young Paul and acted as if she were his mother and not Catherine.

The Empress had ordered the midwife to take the baby and to follow her. Catherine was not to see her child for another month and then on the second time briefly for the churching ceremony. Six months later Elizabeth let Catherine see the child again. The child had in effect become a ward of the state and in a larger sense, the property of the state, to be brought up by Elizabeth as she believed he should be — as a true heir and great-grandson of her father, Peter the Great.

DEATH

In the late 1750s Elizabeth's health started to decline. She began to suffer a series of dizzy spells and refused to take the prescribed medicines. She forbade the word "death" in her presence. Knowing she was dying, Elizabeth used her last remaining strength to make her confession, to recite with her confessor the prayer for the dying and to say good-bye to those few people who wished to be with her including Peter and Catherine and Counts Alexei and Kirill Razumovsky. Finally on 5 January 1762 the Empress died. She was buried in the Peter and Paul Cathedral in Saint Petersburg on 3 February 1762 after six weeks lying in state.

THE COURT OF THE EMPRESS

Under the reign of Elizabeth the Russian court was one of the most splendid in all Europe. Foreigners were amazed at the sheer luxury of the sumptuous balls and masquerades. The Russian court had steadily increased in importance throughout the 18th century and came to hold more cultural significance than many of its Western counterparts due its inclusive nature; any "well to do inhabitants" were welcome at Court. The Court, like most Imperial Courts, was considered a reflection of the ruler at its center and Elizabeth was said to be "the laziest, most extravagant and most amorous of sovereigns." Elizabeth was intelligent but lacked the discipline and early education necessary to flourish as an intellectual; she found the reading of secular literature to be "injurious to health."

She was kind and warm-hearted for the emotion's sake alone, once going so far as to offer to finance the reconstruction of Lisbon after the 1755 earthquake destroyed the Portuguese city despite having and wanting no diplomatic relationship with the nation. She hated bloodshed and conflict and went to great lengths to alter the Russian system of punishment, even outlawing capital punishment.

Even in court this peacemaker spirit made itself evident. According to historian Robert Nisbet Bain, it was one of Elizabeth's "chief glories that, so far as she was able, she put a stop to that mischievous contention of rival ambitions at Court, which had disgraced the reigns of Peter II, Anne and Ivan VI, and enabled foreign powers to freely interfere in the domestic affairs of Russia."

She was also deeply religious, passing several pieces of legislation that undid much of the work her father had done to limit the power of the church. Yet of all her various characteristics manifested in the structure of Court life the most evident were her extravagance, her vanity, and her gaiety and playful nature. The notorious extravagance of Elizabeth came to define the Court in many respects. Elizabeth created a world in which aesthetics reigned supreme, producing a Court in which an understood competition existed amongst courtiers to see who could look best, second only to Her Majesty. As historian Mikhail Shcherbatov stated, her court was "arrayed in cloth of gold, her nobles satisfied with only the most luxurious garments, the most expensive foods, the rarest drinks, that largest number of servants and they applied this standard of lavishness to their dress as well." Clothing soon became the chosen means in Court by which to display wealth and social standing.

Elizabeth is reported to have owned 15,000 dresses, several thousand pairs of shoes, and a seemingly unlimited number of stockings. She was known to never wear a dress twice and to change outfits anywhere from two to six times a day. Since the Empress did this her courtiers did as well.

It is reported that to ensure no one wore a dress more than once to any ball or notably formal occasion, the Empress had her guards stamp each gown with special ink. Men at court were known to wear diamond buttons, own jeweled snuff boxes, and adorn their servants in uniforms made of gold. It was also during her reign that a great number of silver and gold objects were produced, the most the country had seen thus far in its history. Elizabeth's extravagance was also clearly displayed in the foods eaten at Court. It was not unheard of for Elizabeth to order over a thousand bottles of French champagnes and wines at any given time to be served at one event and present pineapple at all of her receptions, despite the difficulty of procuring the fruit in such quantities.

However Elizabeth's incredible extravagance and adoration of exotic goods ended up greatly benefiting the country's infrastructure. Needing goods shipped from all over the postal system roads were modernized in order to fulfill the Empress's many desires. Elizabeth's vanity and the attention paid to her personal appearance also had indelible ramifications on Court life.

Elizabeth as a young woman had been incredibly attractive and, in turn, she desired to be the most attractive amongst any company at all times. In order to ensure this was the case Elizabeth passed various decrees outlining what was acceptable of her courtiers in regards to appearance in relation to the Empress. These edicts included a law against wearing the same hairstyle, dress, or accessory as the Empress. One woman, Natalya Lopukhina, accidentally wore the same item as the Empress and was lashed across the face for her offense. Another law created by Elizabeth was that any French fabric salesman had to first sell to her before attempting to sell to anyone else; those who disregarded this law were arrested. One famous story exemplifying the Empress's vanity is that once Elizabeth got a bit of powder in her hair and was unable to remove it.

She was therefore obligated to cut her hair to rid herself of the splotch and in turn she made all of the ladies at Court do the same, which they did "with tears in their eyes." This aggressive vanity be-

Elizabeth of Russia in a portrait of Louis Tocque (1756)

came a tenet of Elizabeth's Court throughout the entirety of her reign particularly as she grew older. According to the historian Tamara Talbot Rice, "Later in life her outbursts of anger were directed either against people who were thought to have endangered Russia's security or against women whose beauty rivaled her own."

ARTS AND CULTURE AT THE COURT

Despite Elizabeth's volatile, often violent reactions in regards to her appearance, the Empress was ebullient in most other matters particularly when it came to Court entertainment. Elizabeth was renowned throughout and beyond Russia for the balls she held and her fierce commitment to the arts, particularly music, theater, and architecture.

It is reported that Elizabeth threw two balls a week. One would be a large event with an average of 800 guests in attendance, most of whom were the nation's leading merchants, members of the lower nobility, and guards stationed in and around the city of the event.

The other ball was a much smaller affair reserved for Elizabeth's closest friends as well as members of the highest echelons of nobility. These smaller gatherings began as masked balls but evolved into the famous Metamorphoses balls by 1744.

At these Metamorphoses balls, guests were expected to dress as the opposite sex, with Elizabeth often dressing up as Cossack or carpenter in honor of her father.

The costumes not permitted at the event were those of pilgrims and harlequins, which the Empress considered profane and indecent respectively. Most members of court thoroughly disliked these balls since most looked ridiculous but Elizabeth adored them.

As Catherine the Great's advisor Potemkin posited, this adoration was due to the fact that she was "the only woman who looked truly fine, and completely a man... As she was tall and powerful, male attire suited her."

Though the balls were by far her most personally beloved and lavish events, Elizabeth often threw children's birthday parties and wedding receptions for those affiliated with her Court, going so far as to provide dowries for each of her ladies-in-waiting. The other court pastimes most enjoyed by Elizabeth and therefore most revered in Court were theatre, music, and architecture.

The Empress had a longstanding love of theatre and had a stage erected in the palace to enjoy the countless performances she sanctioned. Though countless domestic and foreign works were shown, the French plays quickly became the most popular, often being performed twice a week.

In tandem with Elizabeth's love of theatre, music came to be of high importance in Court. Many attribute its popularity to Elizabeth's relationship with Alexei Razumovsky, a Ukrainian Cossack and the supposed husband of the Empress, who reportedly relished music.

Regardless of the reasoning behind its introduction, Elizabeth transformed "her court into the country's leading musical center." She would spare no expense in its regard, importing leading musical talents from Germany, France, and Italy. As to the Empress's love of architecture, she financed many construction projects during her reign. Her most famous creations were the Winter Palace, which she commissioned and oversaw the construction of but died before its completion, and the Smolny Convent. The Convent, built when Elizabeth considered becoming a nun, was one of the many religious buildings erected at her behest, using the nation's funds (rather than those of the church). According to Robert Nisbet Bain, "No other Russian sovereign ever erected so many churches."

РИСУНКИ

ОДЕЖДЫ и ВООРУЖЕНІЯ

РОССІЙСКИХЪ

ВОЙСКЪ.

PLATES LIST OF ILLUSTRATIONS

436 Oboist, drummer and musician of the Musketeer of the Duchess Regiment, 1756-1761.

437 Oboist and musican of the Musketeer Duchess Regiment, 1761.

438 Musketeeer Officer and soldier of Naryshkin regiment, 1756-1761

439 Banners of the Grenadier Cap and cartridge pouch: Musketeers and Officers, 1756-1761.

440 Grenadier NCO and Officer of the Musketeer Naryshkin Regiment, 1756-1761.

441 Trumpet and Drummer Musketeer Naryshkin Regiment, 1756-1761

442 Soldier and NCO of artillery regiment, 1756-1761.

443 Hat of artillery men. 1756-1762.

444 – 456 Holstein Art. Cartridge pouch. 1756-1762. Palash and Lyadunka of the Life-Dragoon Reg. 1756-1762.

445 Officer and Fifer Artillery Battalion, 1756-1761

446 Grenadier Officer and the Musketeer's Von-Manteuffel Regiment, 1762.

447 The Musketeer Prince William regiment, 1762.

448 Officer of the Musketeer Prince William regiment, 1762.

449 Grenadier Musketeer Prince William regiment 1762 year.

450 Musketeer and Grenadier Musketeer Prince August regiment, 1762 year.

451 Soldier and Officer of the Musketeer Quettenburg Regiment. 1762 year.

452 Grenadier and an Officer of the Musketeer Quettenburg regiment, 1762.

453 Officer and the Grenadier Essen of the Battalion, in 1762.

454 Soldier and Officer of the Grenadier Weiss Battalion of 1762.

455 private of Leib Dragoon Regiment, 1756-1762.

457 NCO of the Life-Dragoon Regiment, 1756-1762.

458 Officer of the Life-Dragoon Regiment, 1756-1762.

459 Grenadier Life-Dragoon Regiment, 1756-1762.

460 Plate of the Gren. Cap and Gren. Cartridge pouch: Off. and NCO of the Leib-Dragoon Reg. 1756-1762.

461 Grenadier Officer of the Life-Dragoon Regiment, 1756-1762.

462 Drummer and Trumpet of Leib-Dragoon Regiment, 1756-1760

463 NCO and private of the Leib-Cuirassier Regiment, 1756-1761.

464 – 467 Cuirass of the Leib-Cuir. Reg., 1756-1762. Ljadunochnaja badge and Cirasses Holstein Cuir. 1756-1762

465 Officer of the Leib-Cuirassier Regiment, in 1756 and 1761

466 Leib-Cuirassier regiment, 1756-1761

468 NCO of the Hussar Regiment, in 1760 and 1761.

469 Officer of the Hussar Regiment, in 1760 and 1761.

470 Lieutenant-Commander of the Life-Dragoon Regiment, 1762.

471 Insignia of the Life-Dragoon Regiment, 1762 year.

472 Sergenat of the Ludwig's Dragoon Prince Dragoon Regiment, 1762.

473 Officer of Dragoon Prince George Ludwig Regiment, 1762.

474 Grenadier and Grenadier Officer Dragoon Prince George Ludwig Regiment, 1762.

475 Soldiers of the Cuirassier Leuven Regiment, 1762.

476 Officers of the Cuirassier Leuven Regiment, 1762.

477 Soldier and Officer of the Cuirassier Lotcova regiment, 1762.

478 Private cuirassier regiment, 1762 year.

479 Officer of the Cuirassier regiment 1762.

480 Hussar Cobeltish Regiment, 1762.

481 Officer of the Cobeltish Hussar Regiment, 1762.

482 Officer and NCO of the Hussar Regiment, 1762.

483 Soldier and NCO of the Fortress Garrison, 1758-1761.

484 Officer of the Fortress Garrison, 1758-1761

485 NCO, private and drummer of the insulated hill, 1756-1761.

486 Officer of the Invalid Corps, 1756-1761.

487 The Garrison Regiment, 1762.

488 Officer Garrison Kruger Regiment, 1762.

489 Officers of the Holstein reg., Leib Dragoon and Musketeer Prince Wilhelm (in frock coats). 1756-1762.

490 Brigadier of the Holstein troops, 1756-1762.

491 General of the Holstein troops, 1756-1762.

492 Holstein General, 1756-1762. In a frock coat.

493 Holstein's Banner, 1762 year.

The Russian Zar Peter III

Musketeers belts and Grenadier cartridge pouch, 1762 year

Musketeer sergeant, in 1762

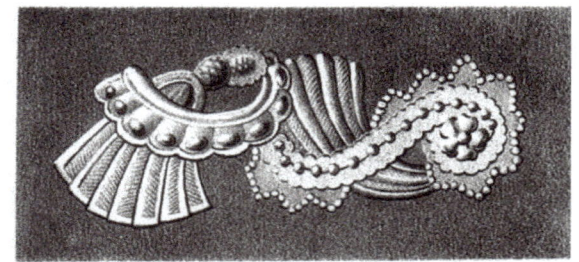
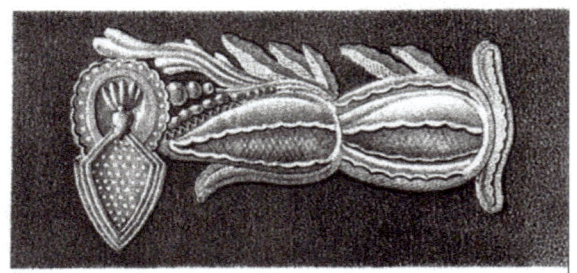

Officer's laces and decorations

26

Officers of the Musketeer Regiment, 1762

Halebard point Army Officers, 1762. Shabraque Army Officers, in 1762.

Halebard point Army Officers, 1762. Shabraque Army Officers, in 1762.

Grenadier, in 1762.

The Grenadier Hat, in 1762

NCO Army Grenadier, in 1762

Plaque on the cap and cartridge pouch of Grenadier Officers, 1762

Auditor, 1762

Auditor, 1762

Auditor, 1762

Auditor, 1762

Auditor, 1762

Sergeant and Field Artillery cannonier, 1762

Officer of Field Artillery, 1762.

408

Musketeer of the Guard, 1762 years

Musketeer: NCO and staff Officers L.G. Preobrazhensky regiment, in 1762.

Hat of the Guards Staff-Officers, 1762

Soldier's cap L.G. Preobrazhensky regiment, in 1762.

411

Grenadier L.G. Izmaylovsky regiment, in 1762.

Grenadier Officer L.G. Semenovsky regiment, in 1762

Soldat and Officer L.G. The Bombardier Battalion, 1762.

Banner of the Musketeer Regiment, 1762. Standard of the Novgorod Cuirassier Regiment, 1762.

Banner of the Musketeer Regiment, 1762. Standard of the Novgorod Cuirassier Regiment, 1762.

Banner of the Guards Infantry Regiments, 1762. Standard L.-G. The Horse Regiment, 1762

Banner of the Guards Infantry Regiments, 1762. Standard L.-G. The Horse Regiment, 1762

Musketeer of Von-Manteuffel Regiment, 1756-1761

419

Holstein Rifle, Metal point and Halberd, 1756-1762.

NCO of the Musketeer Von-Manteuffel Regiment, 1756-1761

NCO of the Musketeer Von-Manteuffel Regiment, 1756-1761

Sponton, Scarf, Sign and the Sword of the Holstein troops, 1756-1762.

Grenadiers Musketeer Von-Manteuffel regiment, 1756-1761 g. (Private soldier and carpenter).

Grenadier mitria of Musketeer Von-Manteuffel regiment, 1756-1762

Grenadier Officer of the Musketeer Von-Manteuffel regiment, 1756-1761.

Officer hat plaque of the Musketeer Von-Manteuffel Regiment, 1756-1762

Musket and cartridge pouch of the Grenadier Officers of the Musketeer Von-Manteuffel Regiment, 1756-1761

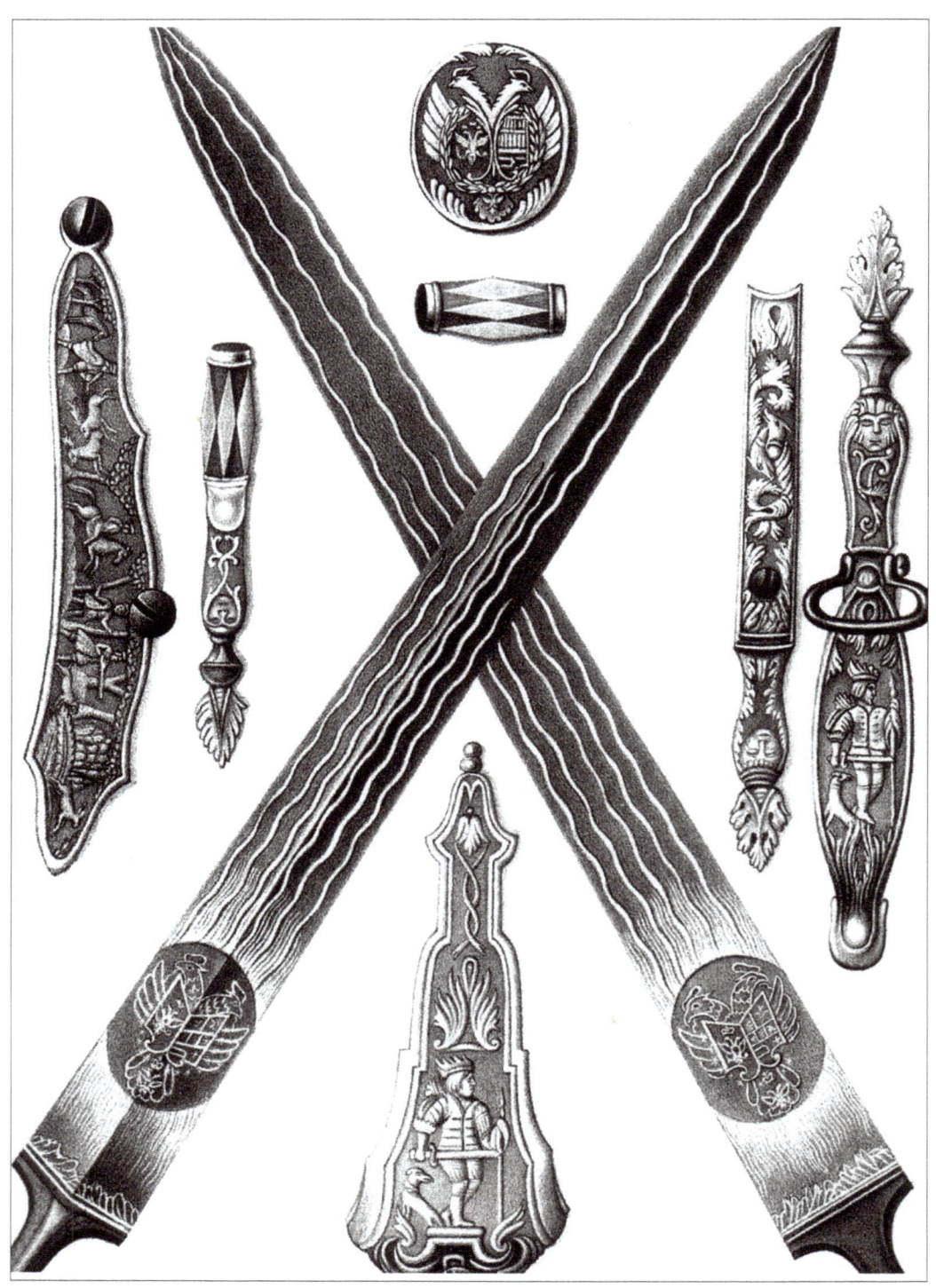

Ornaments on the Holstein Officers' Guns, 1757-1762.

Oboist, drummer and musician of the Musketeer Von-Manteuffel regiment, 1756-1760

The drummer of the Musketeer Von-Manteuffel regiment, in 1761

Musketeer of the Duchess Regiment, 1756-1761

NCO of Musketeer of the Duchess Regiment, 1756-1761.

Officer of the Musketeer of the Duchess Regiment 1756-1761.

Grenadier and Grenadier Officer Musketeer of the Duchess Regiment, 1756-1761

Banners of the Grenadier's cap and Cartridge pouch: Grenadier and Officer of the Musketeer Duchess of the regiment, 1756-1761.

Oboist, drummer and musician of the Musketeer of the Duchess Regiment, 1756-1761

Oboist and musican of the Musketeer Duchess Regiment, 1761.

Musketeeer Officer and soldier of Naryshkin regiment, 1756-1761

Banners of the Grenadier Cap and cartridge pouch: Musketeers and Officers, 1756-1761

Grenadier NCO and Officer of the Musketeer Naryshkin Regiment, 1756-1761

Trumpet and Drummer Musketeer Naryshkin Regiment, 1756-1761

Soldier and NCO of artillery regiment, 1756-1761

Hat of artillery men. 1756-1762

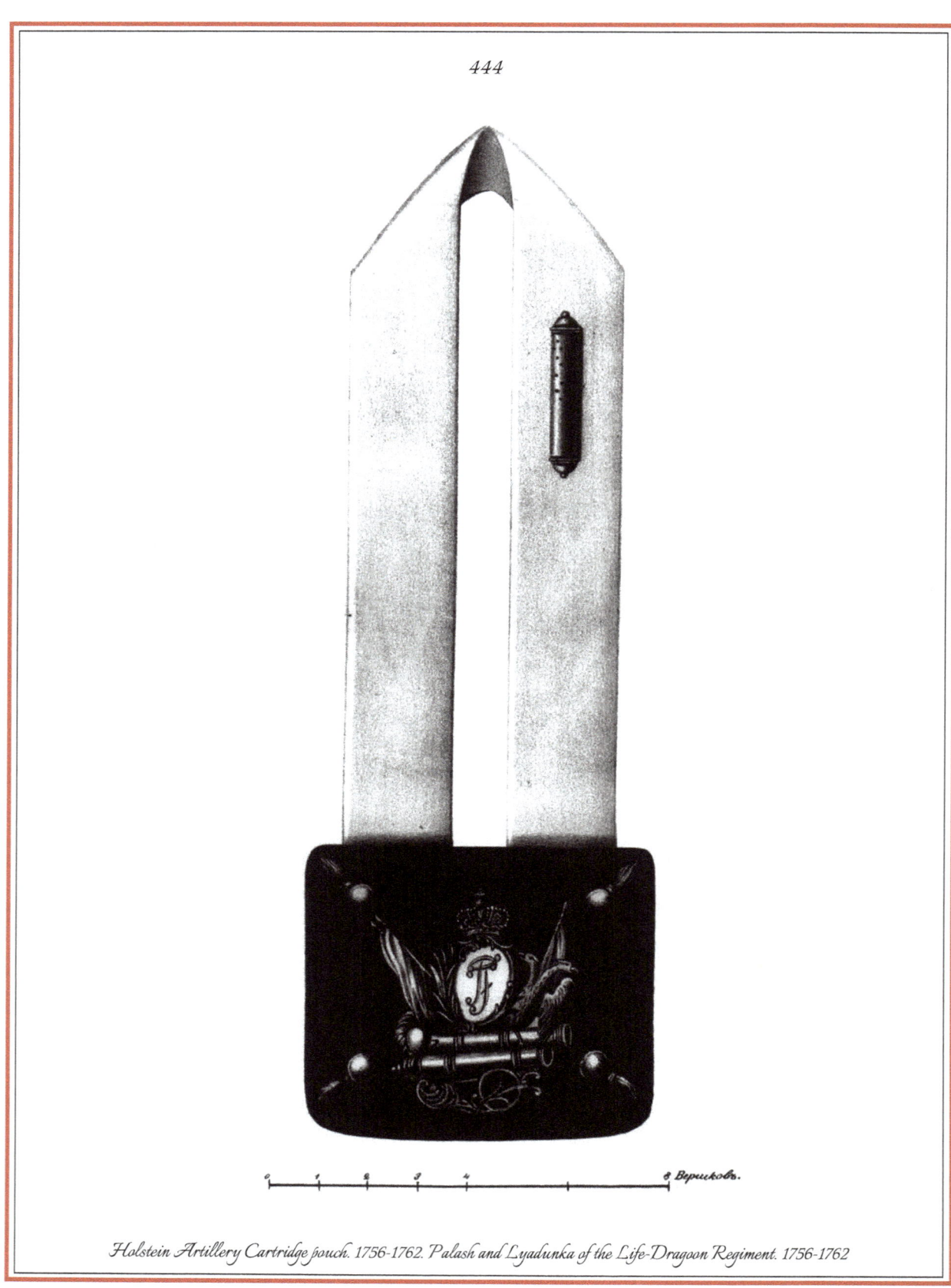

Holstein Artillery Cartridge pouch. 1756-1762. Palash and Lyadunka of the Life-Dragoon Regiment. 1756-1762

Officer and Fifer Artillery Battalion, 1756-1761

Grenadier Officer and the Musketeer's Von-Manteuffel Regiment, 1762

The Musketeer Prince William regiment, 1762

Officer of the Musketeer Prince William regiment, 1762

Grenadier Musketeer Prince William regiment 1762 year

Musketeer and Grenadier Musketeer Prince August regiment, 1762 year

Soldier and Officer of the Musketeer Quettenburg Regiment. 1762 year

Grenadier and an Officer of the Musketeer Quettenburg regiment, 1762.

Officer and the Grenadier Essen of the Battalion, in 1762

Soldier and Officer of the Grenadier Weiss Battalion of 1762.

private of Leib Dragoon Regiment, 1756-1762.

456

Масштабъ къ Лядункѣ.

Масштабъ къ Палашу.

Holstein Artillery Cartridge pouch. 1756-1762. Palash and Lyadunka of the Life-Dragoon Regiment. 1756-1762

NCO of the Life-Dragoon Regiment, 1756-1762

458

Officer of the Life-Dragoon Regiment, 1756-1762

Grenadier Life-Dragoon Regiment, 1756-1762.

Plate of the Grenadier Cap and Grenadier Cartridge pouch: Officer and NCO of the Leib-Dragoon Regiment, 1756-1762.

Grenadier Officer of the Life-Dragoon Regiment, 1756-1762.

Drummer and Trumpet of Leib-Dragoon Regiment, 1756-1760

NCO and private of the Leib-Cuirassier Regiment, 1756-1761

Cuirass of the Leib-Cuirassier Regiment, 1756-1762. Ljadunochnaja badge and Cirasses Holstein Cuirassier, 1756-1762
Insignia of the Life-Dragoon Regiment, 1762 year

Officer of the Leib-Cuirassier Regiment, in 1756 and 1761

466

Leib-Cuirassier regiment, 1756-1761

NCO of the Hussar Regiment, in 1760 and 1761

Officer of the Hussar Regiment, in 1760 and 1761.

Lieutenant-Commander of the Life-Dragoon Regiment, 1762

Sergenat of the Ludwig's Dragoon Prince Dragoon Regiment, 1762

Officer of Dragoon Prince George Ludwig Regiment, 1762

Grenadier and Grenadier Officer Dragoon Prince George Ludwig Regiment, 1762

Soldiers of the Cuirassier Leuwen Regiment, 1762

Officers of the Cuirassier Leuven Regiment, 1762.

Soldier and Officer of the Cuirassier Lotcova regiment, 1762

Private cuirassier regiment, 1762 year.

Officer of the Cuirassier regiment 1762

Hussar Cobeltish Regiment, 1762.

Officer of the Cobeltish Hussar Regiment, 1762

Officer and NCO of the Hussar Regiment, 1762.

Soldier and NCO of the Fortress Garrison, 1758-1761

484

Officer of the Fortress Garrison, 1758-1761

NCO, private and drummer of the insulated hill, 1756-1761

Officer of the Invalid Corps, 1756-1761.

The Garrison Regiment, 1762

Officer Garrison Kruger Regiment, 1762

Officers of the Holstein regiments, Leib Dragoon and Musketeer Prince Wilhelm (in frock coats). 1756-1762

Brigadier of the Holstein troops, 1756-1762

General of the Holstein troops, 1756-1762

Holstein General, 1756-1762. In a frock coat

Holstein's Banner, 1762 year

SOLDIERS, WEAPONS & UNIFORMS ALREADY PUBLISHED
(SOME TITLES)

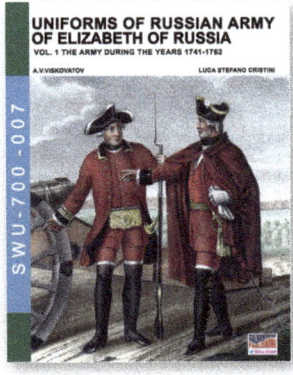

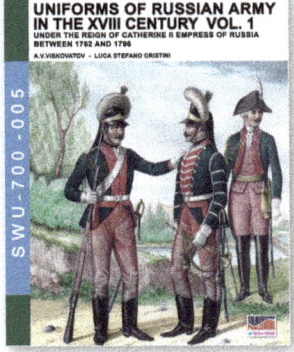

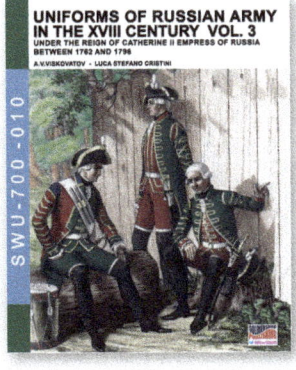

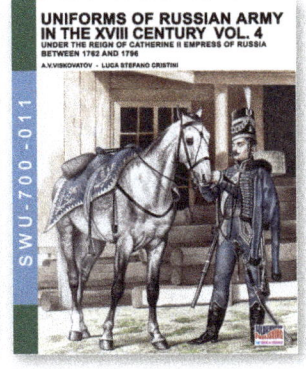

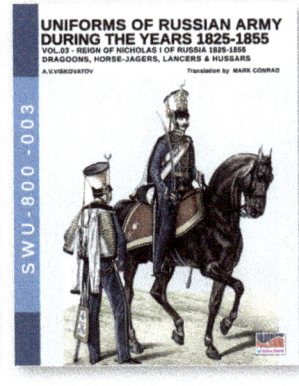

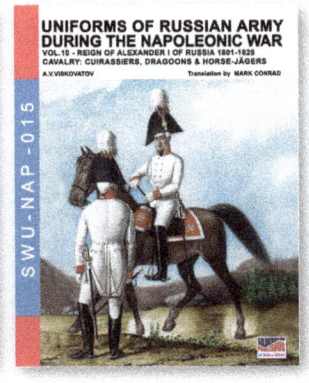

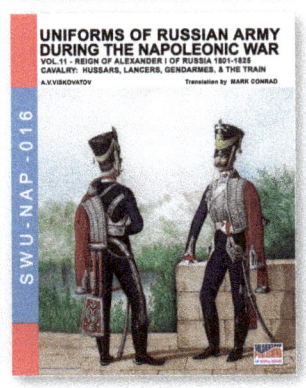